T0209489

A heartwarming, true account of the many trials experienced by the author where GOD shows up and answers prayers.

James 1vs 2.

I have written this book to honour God whom I serve through Christ Jesus. I would like to thank every person who obeyed the Voice of God and helped us along the way. May your sowing be returned to you 100-fold.

I hope and trust that this book will be read and enjoyed by many, and as they read it, people's faith and trust in God will increase. If He can do it for me, He can do it for you as well.

***NB: Revelation 12 vs 13 – Satan is slain by the Word of your testimony and the blood of the Lamb

Thank You Dad

VEE LINDOLENT

WESTBOW
PRESS®
A DIVISION OF THOMAS NELSON
& ZONDERVAN

WestBow Press books may be ordered through booksellers or by contacting:

WestBow Press
A Division of Thomas Nelson & Zondervan
1663 Liberty Drive
Bloomington, IN 47403
www.westbowpress.com
1 (866) 928-1240

All Scripture quotations are taken from the King James Version.

ISBN: 978-1-9736-5212-0 (sc)
ISBN: 978-1-9736-5213-7 (e)

Print information available on the last page.

WestBow Press rev. date: 4/11/2019

Contents

1

Prologue

Where do I start? I guess in the beginning.

For as long as I can remember, I have been a Christian. I recall attending Sunday School at the age of 3 with my siblings. A smile lights up my face as I think about the annual family picnics where we received our Christmas gifts from our Sunday School teachers. I loved Sunday School. Then came Church and I was always so bored, however I loved the hymns. I still love singing some of the old songs although most have now been replaced by The Winans, Martha Munizzi, Israel Houghton, Hillsong and other artists who sing glorious songs of praise.

Even though I was bored at Church, I went every Sunday with my aunt and 2 sisters. We would walk to church and back. Now, when I see the distance we walked, I am astonished that we completed it in only 20 minutes. I guess being young and energetic helped 😊. This went on till I was about 15 years old.

1.1 The Cold Years

I call this chapter "The Cold Years", because I rarely attended church during this time. I chose, instead, to read late into the night and sleep in the next morning. Why would I want to go to church anyway? Apart from being bored, the Pastor's monotone made every minute seem like an hour. I did go to church every Good Friday and on Christmas day, however. I guess that, deep within me, I knew the importance of these days and the significance of Jesus being born and dying.

In later years, I was called a "Submarine Christian" by my sister for doing this. She said she called me this as I only surfaced twice a year 😊. For someone who only learnt to swim at the age of 33, I thought staying under water that long was a great achievement! My sense of humour (which rubbed off on me from my husband, Peter) enabled me to always see the funny side of things.

1.2   The Good Years

Peter and I had been married for 7 years, had good jobs and a beautiful little daughter whom we had named Leigh. We travelled, ate out a lot (I love food – both working with and eating it. This is where my true passion lies). We entertained; went for dancing lessons. There was not a care in the world. Life was good and we were happy.

2

The Suddenly

South Africa was very much in the transformational phase in the 1990s and without much warning, in 2001, the Anglo-American Company where I worked, went through a restructuring process and I was retrenched. Fortunately, I received a good retrenchment package.

At the same time, the same was happening at the company where Peter worked and suddenly we were both unemployed. Life was still good because we had all this money. Then God blessed me with another beautiful little girl whom we named Macayle.

Together, Peter and I decided to start a little business selling car accessories. While Peter manned the business, I went back to university and enrolled in the Science & Engineering

Programme. At the end of the year, I obtained As in English, Chemistry and Biology. I excelled and loved studying. I was determined to get my degree.

We met Pastor Burton Rampersat for the first time when he came to pray for my aunt and invited us to church the following Sunday. To support my aunt, we went to church and were made to feel very welcome. The people there were all very friendly and embraced us warmly.

When Daniel, the praise and worship leader, started singing, I remembered why I no longer enjoyed going to church and really thought that he was going to go on and on and could not wait for him to stop. All I wanted to do was to get back home as soon as possible to complete the captivating book that I was reading. This had nothing to do with Daniel, as he is the best Praise & Worship Leader I have come to know and I still enjoy listening to him sing. I just don't think I was up for all that singing that particular day.

Then came the WORD by Pastor Burton and I was hooked.

After the service, we were invited to attend a birthday party later that afternoon. I soon found out that, whenever anyone in the church had a function, the entire congregation was invited as they believe that everyone is FAMILY.

We attended the birthday party that afternoon and church the next Sunday. At this Sunday meeting, Pastor Burton came to me and told me that he had a message for me from God. The message was that God wanted me to start calling Him, "Dad". I was gob-smacked!

I lost my own dad when I was twelve and I missed using that term, "DAD". I think growing up, I abused it. Every time we were disciplined by my mother, I would tell her "I am going to tell Daddy about you". He did not believe in hitting kids. If my siblings and I got into disagreements, I would threaten them by telling them I was going to tell Dad about them.

So, I really missed using this word when he passed on and I always said that, if I could have just one wish, it would be to have my Dad back so that he could taste all the good food that I made and tell me how proud of me he was.

By this time, my cooking had reached another level, with family members praising me and telling me how good my food was. My Dad, too, had always loved good food and taught us the importance of buying quality and not quantity. He was a very good father and a real gentleman. And I really missed him.

Amazingly, the more I started addressing God as "Dad" (which felt quite strange, initially), the void I felt for my biological father started to get smaller and smaller and is there no more 😊.

Before we knew it, we were hooked by the Word and were attending Church every Sunday as well as on a Monday night.

I guess this was perhaps just one of times I would experience God's great sense of humour.

When Peter and I got married, we decided we needed to go to church. Peter did not want to go to the church I belonged to for he did not like the "Happy Clappy Church", as he called it. This resulted in me not liking the Catholic Church, as Peter was Catholic. And yet, today, he tries to clap the loudest and even dances while singing and worshipping!!

I was still not reading my Bible every day. For a couple of years, I had a terrible back pain and I remember lying on my bed, praying and telling Satan to let go of my body, as it belonged to God.

After two weeks of prayer, on the 19th of November, 2003, I felt the gentlest touch in my lower back. I knew something had happened. For the first time that morning, I jumped out of bed without an ache.

Only later, when I started to read my Bible, did I find these Words in 1 Corinthians 6 vs 20. This reiterates scripture that tells us if we don't know what to pray for, The Holy Spirit will pray on our behalf.

When I was healed of this back pain, I took all my medication that had been prescribed too. And He did! It's been 14 years now and I have never taken any form of medication. Not that I do not get sick or feel pain. It's just that this is a covenant that

I made with God. Three days max and I am well. If the devil thinks he can break me, he extends it to five days. However, God is my strength and, during these times, I go into overdrive reciting scripture, like Isaiah 53: 5: "By Jesus Stripes, I AM healed".

Peter could not understand how I could bare the pain without taking any medication. He would tell me that doctors are placed there by God for a reason and that I should let them help me. I respect people who seek the services of these doctors, but I expected him to respect my covenant with God.

Then, on 29 August 2012, (I remember the date, as 29 August is my birthday), Peter had suffered a pinched nerve and could barely walk. I could see the pain etched across his face as he struggled to move.

In the early hours of the next morning, I got down on my knees and did not pray for healing over Peter but rather for God to make him understand the covenant that I have with Him.

Peter got up that morning totally pain-free. He has since respected my decision not to take any medication.

3

Back to Business

The business, on the other hand, was struggling. The expenses that the business was incurring were greater than the income it was generating. Soon we found ourselves dipping into our savings more and more to help sustain the business. Before we knew it, we had nothing left in our bank account.

Then, as if this was not bad enough, both our cars packed up at the same time. Peter had a BMW 325i that was not just drinking petrol, it was gulping and guzzling it! No matter what we did, it was perpetually thirsty and we were starting to feel the pinch. I, on the other hand, was driving a Daewoo, which suddenly seemed to be riddled with arthritis!

Little did I know this was to be the start of a period in our lives that I would come to refer to as, our "Valley Period".

I did not believe in having store accounts, however I did have one with Woolworths. I loved shopping there. I must admit that my one weakness in life is shopping. Not for clothes, shoes, jewelry or perfumes, BUT groceries! 😊. You can imagine what my cupboards and fridge looked like.

I had enough food to last me for at least 4 months. I remember one day I opened the freezer and a box of prawns fell out and I said to myself: "Now I can say that Prawns are literally falling out of my fridge!" However, this too started to empty out and soon the fridge was bare.

Peter always teased me that with the amount of money that I spent at Woolies, they should have given me shares (if only they did 😊). I valued my good standing credit and always paid my account on time. Not once did I have a debit returned.

Under the current circumstances, however, I soon found myself unable to make my regular monthly installments and started receiving calls from the accounts department gently reminding me to pay my account. I was so upset with Woolworths! Could they not go into my records and see what a good customer I had been? Surely something must be wrong? But, they don't care, they just wanted what was due to them. I tried to buy time by saying I would pay it the following week. And so it went on…

During this time, we became friends with a gentleman we

met at church named Eddie Candasamy who was in the same cell group as us. Peter and Eddie clicked immediately, and he soon became a regular visitor at our home. The three of us got along really well and we would sit and talk into the early hours of the morning.

We would talk about the Word and he shared with us how his young wife died of cancer and how she praised God right till the end. During this time, I learnt how good avocado with pepper and salt was on toast. We tried to get Peter to try it, but he would not (he now regrets it - yes, you guessed it, he now loves it!).

Anyway, to cut a long story short, it was Eddie who told me to tell Woolworths the truth and arrange a payment plan to settle the account. I did as he suggested and made a promise to myself never to buy anything from Woolworths again (unless it was on sale!). 17 years later, even though I can now afford to shop there, I have kept this promise.

4

Our Spiritual Life
vs the Natural

By now, we were at church six days out of the seven. I oversaw the welfare department. Peter was the "sound man" as well as collecting, counting and signing off on all the monies received during each of the services, which he did together with fellow parishioner, Krish Perumal.

Nobody knew what we were starting to go through and I liked it that way. I remember there was a visiting pastor from India who preached to us at our church one Sunday morning and I will never forget his words. He said: "Sometimes when you are being stripped of everything, God will restore you – with interest" so, "Count it ALL joy for the trials that you go through - James 1 vs 2". Well, it seemed that God was talking directly to me through this preacher. I wrote down this scripture and I always say that it is this scripture that saw me through every trial thereafter. Looking back, I am glad and grateful that I received this Word very early on in our "Valley Period".

The closer we were drawing to God, the stronger our Spirit life was getting and the attack in the Natural became greater. James 1 vs 2 😊

7 years prior to this time, my sister had given me a King James Version Bible as a present. I had kept it in my bedside drawer and it had not seen the light of day. I decided now was the time to start to read the Bible. I read the entire Bible in a month and thereafter attended Bible studies. I have since read the Bible 5 times, start to end and every time I read it, I get new revelations.

Still, the trials never stopped.

I remember it was a Saturday morning in 2004, when I got a telephone call from Telkom telling me that we needed to pay R700 by the Monday morning, otherwise they were going to cut off the telephone service. I put down the telephone and said to God: "DAD, I don't even have R70! Where am I going to get R700?" I then went about my day and completely forgot about the incident.

The next day, we went to church and we learnt that we

should leave whatever baggage is weighing us down at the door, so that we can praise and worship God 200%.

After the service, it is normal for everybody to spend some time chatting to one another and finding out how everyone is doing. I was doing the same when Krish saw me and came up to shake my hand. As he did so, I felt him press something into my hand but did not dare open my hand to see what it was. I had a feeling it was money. I prayed that no one else would come over and shake my hand as this meant that I would have to open my palm and if anyone saw, he or she would know that this money was given to me.

A little later, whilst still outside mingling and chatting, Peter came up to me to tell me that Pastor Burton wanted to see us. We both went to him and he told us that, during the entire service, the Holy Spirit was with him and told him that the church needs to sow into our lives. I thanked him and replied that it was only because he had taught us about sowing, that we will graciously accept it.

He then handed us a sealed envelope which I quickly shoved into my bag and we got into the car. As soon as we got home, I opened the envelope and saw that there was R500 inside and Krish had placed a R100 note into my hand. We decided there and then that we were going to pay R300 towards the phone bill and the rest we were going to use to buy some groceries, which included milk for Macayle.

Our home had always been a place where members of the church could stop by and whatever I had cooked we would share with them. This evening, a couple came by and after an hour, Chris, the husband, called Peter aside and told him that he felt in his spirit that he needs to sow into our lives. He gave Peter a further R100. Peter showed me the R100. Total received that day – R 700.

I immediately remembered back to what I had said to God about where I would get the R700 from! He had provided. I went straight to Peter and told him why the entire R700 must be paid to Telkom.

The next morning, Peter had to ask Eddie for a lift to work as he did not have money for petrol. Eddie stopped at the post office and Peter paid in the R700 for the telephone account.

At the end of the working day, Eddie stopped at the bank to withdraw money, came to the car and told Peter that GOD had told him to give him this, handing over R300. Not only did my "Dad" give me the money for the telephone bill, but he also gave me money for food. This was to be just the first of many instances where GOD provided. It re-iterates the fact that GOD really DOES give you more than you ask for! I started to put all my trust and faith in God. I became like a sponge, absorbing the Word and reading my Bible.

4.1   An Earthly Angel

The Bible teaches us that we must be very careful about the company that we keep. Good friends are gifts from above. I had acquaintances galore and then there was my friend, Nancy. Nancy was the most petite person and loyal friend that I knew. That tiny body possessed the biggest heart.

I often wondered if there was space for the other organs 😌.

For instance, I recall a time, one afternoon when she came to visit and just handed over R1 000, the only explanation being that they had sold their Toyota Venture. She was like that, though – always doing these random things for me – and she still does. She really is more like a sister to me than a friend.

4.2   The Pocket of Potatoes.

I needed to buy a pocket of potatoes but found it to be too expensive when I stopped at a vendor selling potatoes on the road. If I had a pocket of potatoes, I would have food for 2 weeks. I could make different dishes with it. We had now reached a point where we were watching and valuing every cent. This was so far from the days of plenty, when we never thought twice about where the next Rand was coming from. Peter never even wanted to have copper coins in his car and would simply throw them out of the window, hoping that someone who needed them would pick them up and use them. Yet, now here we were holding onto these coins for dear life!

Anyway, Peter told me that he would get a pocket of potatoes from the shopping centre on his way to church later on as it would surely be cheaper than from a roadside vendor. We returned home and Peter decided to go over to Eddie who lived across the road from us. 15 minutes later, he came back carrying a pocket of potatoes.

It turned out that Eddie had come across a gentleman selling potatoes at a reasonable price and had bought 2 pockets – one for us and one for himself. All I can say is that I stood in the centre of the kitchen and cried. Once again, God knew what I needed and He provided – despite the fact that I hadn't even asked Him for it!

4.3   The Re-Union

My senior high school years found me in a class with the greatest bunch of humans. Some I knew since childhood. Brilliant minds who have achieved much since leaving school. And here was I, incomplete studies, penniless, with empty cupboards and two unreliable cars.

I received an invite to our class reunion but was telling myself every reason why I should not go. Peter wanted us to go as he had been to a previous class reunion of mine and saw the bond between all, teachers included.

By this time in my journey, I was talking to God all the time, addressing HIM as dad. I told HIM why I did not want to go. What if I was asked what am I doing? What if the car did not work on that day? I really felt like such a LOSER.

Then, in the quiet of the day, having just spent time with God, and now lying on my bed, I heard this audible voice say to me:" Yes, these people may be achievers but how many of them can say they know Me Personally?". With that, I jumped up and decided then and there that I was attending this Re-Union after all. I felt like I was the Highest Achiever because I knew God personally and He had asked ME to call HIM DAD. We conversed daily and HE loves me.

We went to the reunion and here I experienced what I term, "Daniel in the Lion's Den". Not one person asked Peter and I what we were doing for a living. That was God.

Through these trying times, I experienced the peace that surpasses all human understanding. I would put my head on the pillow at night and be out in a second. Then get up the next morning and tell Gos how much I love HIM. This is something that I still do every morning. During this time, I found myself also saying: "Dad, I do not know what trials will come my way today, but I will count it as ALL joy". This became my daily mantra.

4.4 Two Aunts and 2 Brothers

Getting back what the devil had stolen did not happen overnight. It was a journey that saw us operate from a platform of Godly wisdom, faith and trust. Gone were the days of lavish spending on unnecessary items. We tried to manage our finances as best as we could but getting out of that clay we were mired in, did not leave us with much at the end of the month.

I am blessed to still have my mum's sister, Sylvia, (affectionately called Lala) still alive.

A little about Lala: She, together with my mum's youngest sister, Molly, lived with us and helped raise us for long as I can remember. Lala is a retired nurse. When she was a young nurse, she moved to Johannesburg to further her studies. This ensured that she could earn more to help her two sisters and their children. She also took care of Molly and provided for her. Lala would help me wherever she could.

Then there was Peter's dear aunt, Ann Goodwin, who resides in Canada. An extremely bubbly human being, you would never say she is in her 70's. She still has heaps of energy and a sense of jolliness that you just cannot help but love. Many times, she was Spirit lead to sow into our lives.

My eldest brother, Krish, was and still is there whenever I need him. As a 19-year-old, he took on the responsibility of a father's role when my dad graduated to Heaven. He would give my mother most of his salary to help run the house.

Then there was my brother Ravi and his dear wife, Pam. They couriered three large boxes of groceries to me, totally unaware of our situation. In it was everything I needed, from the best olive oil to toiletries.

Both my brothers never knew our need at that time but responded to the call of God.

5

September 2007

Peter relocated to Cape Town in September 2007 while I carried on working as a Purchasing Manager in Durban till the end of December 2007. In my quiet times and after work, I would Google places to rent and send the details over to Peter who then, together with Garth, would go out and view them. At that time the price of houses and the cost to rent were ridiculously high. It was not exactly what you would call a buyers' market.

One of the first things Peter did when he got to Cape Town though, was to look for a church that he could join. A month later, Pastor Burton came down and ministered at Bethel AOG and Peter accompanied him there. According to Peter it felt like being back at Judah where he was surrounded by a warm and very welcoming bunch of people.

5.1   The House and Car

The months flew by and we still had no accommodation. I am told that it was just "by chance" that Peter & Garth saw this house (I do not believe in chances, I believe it was GOD ordained). Anyway, they liked the look of the house and enquired about it. They then put in a bid of much less than what was being asked for. This was a strong, but old house and there was a lot to be done.

The estate agent said that she did not think the owners would accept that low an offer, though. When Peter told me that, all I said was, "That's what she says, but God has the final say." Not long after that, he received a call informing him that our offer had been accepted. We then applied for a bond with the bank.

Peter came up to Durban in mid-December for Christmas. The bank still had not approved the bond. The peace of God still reigned, however, and I believed with all my heart that HE would come through for us. I rested in God.

We also found we had no money for a deposit on the house, but Garth very kindly paid a deposit of R250 000 on our behalf which allowed for the bond that we had applied for to go through.

We will always be eternally grateful to Garth for doing this for us. We needed to leave Durban on the 6th of January 2008 as Peter needed to be back at work on the 8th.

By this time, we had sold the BMW and had only my faulty car which would never have made the 1600km back to Cape Town. Cash was still tight. Peter suggested he drive and we fly. I rejected this as I felt we should all travel together and the thought of him being alone on this long journey did not sit well with me. South Africa was becoming a country where accidents and car hijackings were on the increase.

After much praying, we decided to go and sign for a new car. This was two days before we were scheduled to leave. The salesman had to apply for a loan with the bank. There was NO guarantee that it was going to be approved. We once again just put all our faith and trust in God and at 4 pm the day before we had to leave, everything was sorted out. My GOD!!

Our furniture was to be collected a week after we left. During the time of packing, I also cleaned out what I did not need and sowed it to those that did. I donated a fridge and a table with 4 chairs to our church.

The next morning, the great trek began. All we took were 2 pots, some linen, towels and a few items of clothing each.

We reached our destination at 02:00 am but got lost in the area 😊. We drove around an extra hour trying to find the estate agent's house to collect the keys to the home which God had provided for us. Entering the house, we were pleasantly surprised to notice that the previous owners had left us an oak table and 4 chairs. Amazing, isn't it? We sowed, and God provided. There was also a queen size bed and a gas stove. Isn't God Great?

The next morning, Garth and his dad brought us a little fridge to use. We had the essentials.

5.2   A Job for Me

I got the kids sorted out for school and started to look for a job. I handed in my CV at a recruitment agency. Within a few days, I was called in for an interview. A few days later, I was contacted to start a temporary job and told it is was a highly confidential job in the Procurement Department at a multi-billion rand international company.

Well, the next day, I put on my best dress and my Froggie shoes and off to work I went. I was lead into a little filing room where I had to sit on a cardboard box and sort through hundreds of files, sorting out documents by date. A pair of jeans, T-shirt and takkies would have been more appropriate.

The rate was good, though. More than I'd earned in my previous job, so I tackled this job with all the enthusiasm I could muster, telling myself that I was working for God. It took me two weeks to complete this task. During this time, I observed the culture of the company and its people and I really liked what I saw and felt. I loved the guiding principles. Driving home, I had a conversation with my DAD and told him that I would really like to work at this company permanently.

6

The Waiting Period & My Mum

A while after this, my mother, Queenie, became gravely ill. Everyone thought she was going to die. She even had to wear an oxygen mask. Early one Sunday, we went to church in Landsdowne. My aunt chose to stay at home waiting for an update on my mum.

At church, I know I just cried and cried, begging God to spare my mother as I knew that she needed to let go of certain bitterness that she had built up against the church. You see, when my dad was alive, people from the church were always in and out of our house - from Pastors to Sunday school teachers. When it was time to sing Christmas carols in the area, nobody could wait to reach our house, because my mother would have cooked and baked the entire day and would have set out two long tables filled with all sorts of tasty things, inviting them all to come and eat.

Then my dad passed on and my mum was left a young widow, 39 years old, with 8 kids. Nobody from the church visited her or asked if she needed any help. She was a housewife and had never had a job or worked a day in her life. She became very bitter towards the church for abandoning her in her hour of need.

So, the thought of her passing away now was scary for me, as I know that bitterness can prevent one from entering Heaven. That is why my cry to God was so great. But God stopped and listened. When we got home, I was told that my mother was up, eating and speaking. That is only my God.

7

Back To Work

It had been two months since I had told God that I wanted to work in the billion-dollar company and then, out of the blue, I received a call from the Recruitment Agency and was informed that there was a temporary job available at the same company I'd previously done a stint at. I immediately accepted it and just two months into my job, the lady I was helping resigned and the position became permanent. However, I would still need to apply for it.

At that time, I reported to the consumer director. He also asked me to apply and so I did. I remember before going in to face a panel of interviewers, I prayed and said: "Holy Spirit, you speak for me as I rest in God".

I later received a call from the HR business partner who

congratulated me on how well I'd answered all their questions 😊. I smiled knowing it was my Helper who spoke through me that impressed her. The job was mine. Another special gift from my DAD.

The first thing I did was start a Christian fellowship at work. The first day this was scheduled for, no one turned up and I remember standing alone in this boardroom, waiting. Then I remembered I was not alone. There were angels around, God was there and I started ministering the word that I had prepared. If anyone had been watching me, they would have thought I was insane. Not far from the truth though, I was insane – insane for Christ.

The following week, the room was full.

8

The Fridge

A little while later, the fridge had started to freeze up. Every morning there was water all over the floor. It wasn't very nice to mop up, especially on cold, rainy winter's days. I told my Dad that I needed a new fridge, but I did not want to buy it on account. I wanted to pay cash.

Peter's dad who'd came to visit, saw the need and promised to buy us a fridge, but he never did. Eventually, one Saturday we went to Game and saw a fridge with a Stand-up freezer that I really liked. It was R11 000. Still too much. I complained and said so to my Dad.

The Monday, walking down the corridor at work, I picked up the morning paper and I saw the same fridge for R7 500 at Macro. I immediately called up Game as I am aware of their policy which states that if any other store has the same product for less, they will better the price. They worked out the price that I could get the fridge for and said that I could pay R7300. I was ecstatic! Peter had an investment and he was paid a dividend of R7300. Again, my DAD! Jehovah Jireh. The lesson learnt here was not to put our trust in man, but only and always in God.

9

A God Sent Gardener

When God created Man, He instructed him to take care of the Earth. We were blessed to have been given a luscious garden with the house. It had orange trees, the sweetest mangoes, creamiest of avocados, lemons, and paw-paws. Mr. Kruger, the gentleman we had bought the house from, was really Mr. Green Fingers. Peter, on the other hand, was so far from being Mr. Green Fingers that he even killed the cactus! 😊.

We decided we needed a gardener, but we were wary of getting just anyone. Crime was on the increase and we had been warned to be careful whom we hire. Again, the words came back to me - make your requests known to God – and so that is what we did.

Early one morning, Peter was taking out the bin when a

man approached him to ask if he could leave a settee that he had picked up on the side of the street in our yard. He promised to collect it in the afternoon on his way back from work. Peter allowed him to do this.

In the evening when he arrived to collect his goods, he informed us that he was a refugee from Zimbabwe and was seeking employment as a gardener. Immediately we engaged his services. He was such a good guy. I take delight in telling everybody how God sent me a gardener by the name of *Given*, a Christian, who also loved the Lord.

10

Leigh

Leigh is the eldest of my 2 children. During her grade 12 year, I would get up every day at 4 am to help her study. We would start off with prayer, submitting to God and asking the Holy Spirit to bring to remembrance ALL that I had learnt at school so that I could teach Leigh. We did not have monies for extra tuition.

I went through Mathematics, Physics, Biology and English with her. Our friend, Keagan Thomas, offered to give her free tuition for Mathematics and Physics. Every Sunday, after church, he was at our home. No one had to remind him, he was always on time.

We applied to all the universities in the Western Cape. The examination began, and Leigh passed all her subjects, however, no acceptance at any of the universities. I could see her disappointment and felt for her.

Applications were closed countrywide, and I remember telling her: "Let's pray and apply to the University of Kwa Zulu Natal." We did this and put our trust in God.

I usually get up at 2 am every morning and spend time with God. This Monday morning was no different, however this time, my conversation with God was more intense. I told HIM what was laden in my heart concerning Leigh and I knew that He could make the impossible happen. Jeremiah 32 vs 27: "I am the GOD of the Human Race, is there anything too difficult for me?". I gave Him back scripture as I knew that God watches over HIS Word so that He can perform it. I cried and prayed and then rested in HIM. This lasted for 4 hours. I went back to bed at 6 am for a short nap, got up, showered and went to work.

At this time, I was also meeting with and helping one of my colleagues, a lady by the name of Ilana. I met with Ilana every morning at 9 am to pray for her and help her in her journey in getting to know God. This lasted for 15 minutes. At 9:15 am, Leigh called me on my mobile to ask me if I had seen the email she had sent me. I said No, as I was not at my desk. Excitedly, she told me that she had received an acceptance from The University of Kwa Zulu Natal to study Forensic Science/ Criminology!

I should not have been astounded but I was. She then told me that she had just been informed, via email, that the application was closed with regard to her second option. By the time I got back to my desk 5 minutes later, she had received an acceptance for her second choice as well. All I can say is that there is Nothing That God Cannot Do!

Leigh is now completing her Honours Degree and still studies diligently to show herself approved unto God. I believe God is going to open doors for her that NO man will be able to close.

11

2018 - The Broom Room

In October this year, we found out about a young lady at work who needed to receive prayers for healing. Initially, you could sense she had distanced herself from God, yet we ministered to her and, 2 weeks later, together with Juadene, my prayer warrior partner, we lead her to Christ in the "Broom Room".

11.1 November 2018 – Make Your Requests Known to God.

I needed tiling to be done at home and all the quotes that I received were overpriced. I mentioned this to God and told Him my budget. Peter and I so badly wished that the guy that did our tiling when we moved into our house was still around.

But, we had no contact number for him and neither did we know where he lived.

This was on 10 November. On 16 November at 10:32 pm, I sent a WhatsApp message to a tiler that I had been referred to, asking him whether he could assist us with our tiling. He replied by asking me how big the job was as he had to plan when he could do it, since he already had other jobs lined up.

At about 7:30 am, on 17 November, Jet, my German Shepherd, started to bark continuously. When I checked to see what or who was causing him to bark, I saw it was the tiler who had previously done our tiling. It had been 5 years since we had seen him last, and he wanted to know if I had any work for him. He went on to tell me that he was somehow "drawn" to the house and even wondered if we still stayed there.

I told him that it was God that had brought him back to us and went on to tell him of the conversation I'd had with Peter just a week earlier. I even showed him the message I sent to the other tiler. When he gave me a quote, it was within my budget.

11.2 December 2018 - The Blessings of God NEVER cease

I love December as I love celebrating Christmas. This year I needed to go to Durban, my hometown, for the wedding of my niece, Kim. It was also an opportunity to spend time with family especially my aunt who helped raise us and supported as financially when my Dad passed on.

Juadene, who saw me searching for tickets, offered to buy my ticket on her airmiles. As much as I insisted she should not, she did and told me that she was sowing into my Life.

Unbeknownst to me, she was praying to God to make it possible for Peter to get a ticket the same way. Little did she know that, as she was praying, God was wanting to talk to Biwalya and prepare her for what Juadene was going to ask her the next morning.

When she was in Zambia, an unknown gentleman had walked into her office and told her every time she gets up in the early hours of the morning, God wants to talk to her. After a very long time she awoke twice on the same morning that Juadene was praying to God for this. In Juadene's recount of this, she told us that she asked God to show her who she should ask, and He showed her "B's" face.

Well the next morning, when Juadene went to tell her that

she was there on God's direction, B just sat back, dumbstruck and finally realised why she had woken up twice. She purchased Peter a ticket on the airmiles she had accumulated.

God is good. He is the same yesterday, today and forevermore

12

January 2019: Carol-Ann Savosnick

I firmly believe that GOD puts the right people in place at the appointed time so that His perfect will over our lives can come to fruition.

On the 12 January 2019, I was a guest at The Chuckle n Chirp Toastmasters Club in Somerset West and got chatting with Carol-Ann Savosnick, a long-time member of this club. I mentioned to her that I needed a pair of "Fresh Eyes" to read my book to pick up any errors that I may have overlooked and asked her if she knew any editors?

Well, once again I stand in awe of God. Carol mentioned that she is a proofreader and editor at her company called Edit it Write. She gave me her business card and requested that I send her my manuscript and then she would send me a quote on what she would charge me to proofread my draft.

I did so the next day and I was pleasantly surprised when she returned my draft with a note to say that after reading this book, she was glad to offer her services at No Charge. God only gives us the best as I have found Carol to be a brilliant proofreader and editor and her guidance is truly amazing.

Little does Carol know that when I received her message, I was so moved because, when I started writing this book, God's message to was me that whoever reads this book will be touched and transformed. I believe Carol was certainly touched by it when she read it.

Here is an extract from Carol's reply to me: "I will not charge you anything for editing your book. I believe this is the Word of God and it needs to be put out there."

13

Me

Sadly, despite wanting to further my Bible Studies this year, there have been many reasons that I have been unable to do so. I told God that I will diligently study the Bible and the Holy Spirit needs to be my teacher. I do this every morning. It is amazing that most times, God gives me the Word before it is even preached in Church. I guess it is my Dad's way of telling me: "He is my source for ALL things".

I have been invited to speak at Women's Day conferences and have even had the opportunity to share the Word at several different Churches.

When I think of that "Valley Period" and the many trials that we went through at the time, I find myself saying: "It was

Worth it, for it was during this time that I formed a personal relationship with God through Christ Jesus, which I might otherwise never had had the opportunity to do."

I Love you DAD! I think YOU ARE AMAZING!

Printed in the United States
By Bookmasters